Also by Denise Riley

POETRY

Marxism for Infants

No Fee, *with Wendy Mulford*

Dry Air

Stair Spirit

Mop Mop Georgette

Selected Poems

Say Something Back

PROSE

War in the Nursery: Theories of
the Child and Mother

'Am I That Name?': Feminism and the
Category of Women in History

The Words of Selves: Identification,
Solidarity, Irony

Impersonal Passion: Language
as Affect

Time Lived, Without Its Flow

DENISE RILEY

Denise Riley (signature)

PICADOR

First published 2012 by Capsule Editions

This revised edition first published 2019 by Picador
an imprint of Pan Macmillan
20 New Wharf Road, London N1 9RR
Associated companies throughout the world
www.panmacmillan.com

ISBN 978-1-5290-1710-6

1 3 5 7 9 8 6 4 2

A CIP catalogue record for this book is available from the British Library.

Typeset by Palimpsest Book Production Ltd, Falkirk, Stirlingshire
Printed and bound by CPI Group (UK) Ltd, Croydon, CR0 4YY

Visit **www.picador.com** to read more about all our books
and to buy them. You will also find features, author interviews and
news of any author events, and you can sign up for e-newsletters
so that you're always first to hear about our new releases.

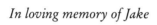

In loving memory of Jake

CONTENTS

Introduction by Max Porter: 1

Time Lived, Without Its Flow 11

Two weeks after the death: 20

One month after the death: 21

Five months after: 23

Six months after: 26

Nine months after: 29

Ten months after: 30

Eleven months after: 35

Sixteen months after: 39

Two years after: 42

Two and a half years later: 43

Two years and ten months later: 54

Three years after: 54

Postscript: 55

Acknowledgements: 85

Endnotes: 87

INTRODUCTION

I wouldn't dare summarize this extraordinary book, or claim any definitive understanding of it. I can only tell you a bit about how I came to read it, and what it did for me.

I had written a short novel about grief. One of its central conceits was that two siblings who had lost a parent would speak in one voice, for each other, against each other, in a state of play. A language game of ever-mourning. For them, time was unfixed. Their childhoods, their growing into teenagers then adults, their notional futures as parents and as dead men themselves, this was all present in the nowness of their storytelling.

These children were an autobiographical device. I

had been trying to find a way of writing about what it is like to lose a parent. About growing up in cahoots with my time-travelling co-conspirator (my brother) along our illusory and twisting lateral axis, backwards and make-believe-forwards, about what seemed like a distinct way we had of seeing other people, granted to us by the absence. To us it seemed like we had our own time and our own sight, defined by what we shared. And I had wanted to write about that, in attempt to better grasp it.

I had been to interview the poet Alice Oswald. Afterwards, she read my novel and wrote to me. She said she had identified in the book some truth, as regards grief:

'I'm not really a fiction reader so the first thing I look for in any writing is its truth . . . I'm interested in the being of grief not the feeling of grief.'

She asked if I had read Denise Riley's essay on a-temporality, on mourning and time. I hadn't. All I knew of it was that it related to the astonishing poem 'A Part Song', which had appeared in the *London Review of Books* in 2012.

'A Part Song' was a piece one doesn't forget

reading. It is a long poem about maternal grief. It is about elegy, but rages against the elegiac mode, and takes its reader on an extraordinary journey. It is profoundly tender, and breathtakingly candid.

A few weeks later *Time Lived, Without Its Flow* arrived.

I found that it was an essay about the being of grief. Its subject therefore is not death, but arrested time. Riley's project is to describe and interrogate 'that acute sensation of being cut off from any temporal flow after the sudden death of your child.'

It is an essay about minutes, hours, days, weeks, months and years.

It is also an essay which gathers into itself the poetry, philosophy and *being grief* of others.

After reading it, I sat for some time with the small book in my hands marvelling that so few pages could have such an impact, could contain so much. I felt sure that I had emerged from the final pages quite changed, and I was grateful. A reader is changed by any text, but here the alteration felt fundamental. I felt I might never read poetry the same way again, and I felt I finally had some clarity about what

3

happens to us who are still here when someone is suddenly gone. I can think of only a handful of works of art which have had such an instantaneous and welcome impact upon me. Truthfully, I might have thrown my own book in the bin had it not already gone to the printers.

Later, I discovered that *Time Lived, Without Its Flow* is one of those books that has been handed from reader to reader like a secret. And indeed in those first moments after reading I was already listing future readers in my mind. People with whom I'd discussed some of the themes Riley touches on. People whose strong reactions to other very dramatic analyses of grief suggested they might welcome this altogether more candid, pointedly undramatic approach. This rigour and what it generates in the feeling reader.

Many people have told me that they were looking for something – as the poet who doesn't read much fiction was looking for truth – and that they found it in this essay. I feel the same. Simply put, I was looking for a literary account of bereavement which did more than recreate or reshuffle existing (at best inadequate or boring, at worst idiotic or hopelessly sentimental) ways of writing about grief. I was looking for non-fiction burnished to the point of poetic intensity. I was looking for writing that carried in the very texture of its lines the remade relationship between a person gone and a person remaining. Not *about* grief, but fashioned *of it* and *for it*.

I was looking for a single line as good as this:

'I work to earth my heart.'

The overwhelming characteristic of this essay is brilliant exactitude. It has such an absence of writerly mannerism or manipulation that one feels one is being looked in the eye and must not turn away. There is no game as there sometimes is when the essay form is used as a gymnastic floor display of a writer's talents or bibliography. There is just a person getting on with the job she has set herself and never once flinching or hiding behind any authorial scenery. It has the focused clarity of a recitation. The essay shares its process with us, and invites us to experience time with it, but it is also quite private. It is profoundly powerful without so much as a whiff of melodrama. As with Riley's poems, one needs to read certain lines over and over because of the sheer quality and complexity of the thinking within. Like her poems, there is a gorgeous no-nonsense technical virtuosity while dealing with strange and painful things. Like her poems she arrives at achingly beautiful conclusions without ever employing familiar, kitsch, or syrupy emotive strategies.

Reflecting on the 'paucity of accounts' of the arrested time she is experiencing, Riley asks: 'Wherever is the literature – for it must exist, it's needed – that deals closely with this strange arresting of time?'

My pulse quickened when I read this. This had been my question too. My obsessive question. And her asking is so deftly personal, and so clear, it reminds me (this can't be coincidence, or a wishful trick of tonal transference) of my mum. And of my grandmother. It is a way of speaking that is part and parcel of maternal authority and experience. It both subtly contains and moves past a vocabulary of pain in the same quick gesture. It's the brisk sureness of 'it must exist' combined with the open-hearted simplicity of how much it is 'needed'. How unusual to state so calmly in a critical context what is *needed*. It struck me as deliciously un-English (as jouissance is, as analysis is?). And it struck me as absolutely correct. 'Yes!' I felt like screaming, 'See? We need it!' How startling and unusual is Riley's singular manner of essayism, which balances desire and theoretical rigour so generatively. It's deep mastery. And then there's her answer, which is to go on and make it. A literature of consolation. To create what doesn't exist. Through and with poetry, because it is poetry that best deals with the 'serious problems of what's describable'.

Here in this book you hold in your hands are some of the best pages I've ever read on what poems are, on the 'literature of consolation, what that could be or what it might do'.

Underlined by pencil in my copy, Riley writes of a Wordsworth quatrain: 'Between these stanzas there's a heavy crash of altered time.'

What a gorgeous thing. Up and into my own emotional universe comes this 220-year-old poem, fresh and brand new. Heaved up and set to walking by the rhythm and energy of Riley's use of it. She unlocks and shows us the poem in the way Helen Vendler might unlock a line of Dickinson, or T. J. Clark might show us how a Giotto works. It is the scalpel-fine touch of a literary surgeon. And that Riley has turned this sharp tool on herself, on the writer in the world reckoning with classical agony the no-return of her son, means that this is literary criticism as love, and I have always hoped such a thing might exist, just as the poet hoped truth in fiction might exist. And Riley shows us how, in what ways, tentatively or objectively, this must be a maternal project. A continuation of the relationship she had with a living son. She shows us that the 'time of the dead is, from now on, contained within your own.' Her son's time is her own. What a wonderful idea. What a vital corrective to banal narratives of 'moving on', this radically un-deathly conception of an altered life. What a promise this might be to the living, that we will contain their time within our own once they are gone. 'Time *is* the person', she writes. How much brighter, wilder and more essential this feels as a formation than any 'blandly containing' concept of mourning.

I was profoundly moved when I read these pages. In contemplating Riley's hesitant portrait of a maternal temporality, I wondered if I might begin to grope my way towards a paternal or fraternal way of holding the still living and the dead together, enduringly related. Sharing time. I understood that this might not necessarily be an esoteric or rarefied thing, or even a literary thing, but a straightforward, domestic thing. A manifestation of care. I could see a way to think it through. Riley's essay is a permission giver. Each reader runs off with it, like Tom into the garden after the clock has struck thirteen. Ghost siblings, parents, friends, grandparents, the distant lives of others. The grief of groups, of nation states. From such a stunningly compelling analysis, for each of us, a way of being in the broken clock of the world might emerge. In times of spasmodic political upheaval, or extremism of opinion on national matters, I always think of Riley's transpersonal 'generational temporalities'. In Riley's delicate formation we might mourn better. We might speak to each other and make sense of things better if we know better how we are living with the dead.

This is not a sweet book, or an easy book, but I consider it to be a radically kind book.

At the start of 'A Part Song', Riley asks: 'You principle of song, what are you *for* now . . .'

I have sat with this book, and with Riley's poems, and I have felt the critical sometimes angry dead read with me, and I have thought slantwise and differently about myself and them, and others, and seen light in areas I had wanted to be flooded dark. And I have rejoiced and rushed to share the song with others. That is what it's for.

Max Porter, 2019

Time Lived, Without Its Flow

I'll not be writing about death, but about an altered condition of life. The experience that not only pre-occupied but occupied me was of living in suddenly arrested time: that acute sensation of being cut off from any temporal flow that can grip you after the sudden death of your child. And a child, it seems, of any age.

Because I'm considering a state that's not rare, but for many is lived daily, I shan't be having recourse to an exceptionalist diction of 'trauma'. And whether this state might be considered to fall within the compass of 'pathology' doesn't greatly bother me here, although my inclination's to avoid that judgement. Certainly someone could produce an account of this freezing of time as an act of dissociation, or a borderline psychotic effort to erect a shield against the death's reality. Or someone else could produce neurological accounts of the brain flooded with its own – this time, biochemical – defences. But I want to avoid offering my amateur speculations about existing theories. Instead, while hoping not to lapse into melodrama or self-regarding memoir, I'll try to convey that extraordinary feeling of a-temporality.

But how could such a striking condition ever be voiced? It runs wildly counter to everything that I'd thought we could safely assume about lived time. So this 'arrested time' is also a question about what is describable; about the linguistic limits of what can be conveyed. I'm not keen on conceding to any such limits. Yet it seems that the possibilities for describing, and the kinds of temporality that you inhabit, may be intimately allied. For there do turn out to be 'kinds', in the plural.

This stopping of time can, for those who find themselves plunged into it, be lived. It turns out, surprisingly, not to be necessary to live only inside a time that runs in a standard movement. You discover, on the contrary, that you can manage well enough inside your private non-time of pure stasis. That such an experience is not uncommon, I'm sure, as I've listened closely for several years to what bereaved parents say in meetings, in online discussions, or in private encounters – and this in two countries. Yet any published mention of this seemingly a-temporal life is rare. Before speculating about its absence, I want to insist that such a prolonged cessation of the flow of time is not contained by the well-worn metaphorical remark that 'time stopped'. There's nothing that feels either familiar or metaphorical in living out this condition in which time, perhaps for years on end, is arrested. The weak metaphor of 'time stopped' would sap the force from a description of this new state. Once you're plunged into it, the actual metaphoricity of our usual accounts of the passage of time is laid bare, for now you realize that the real espousal of figurative speech would be to maintain that time inevitably 'flows'.

Hard to put into words, yet absolutely lucid as you inhabit it daily, this sensation of having been lifted clean out of habitual time only becomes a trial if you attempt to make it intelligible to others who've not experienced it. The prospect of recounting it in a written form stayed, for me, both repugnant and implausible for well over two and a half years after the death. You can't, it seems, take the slightest interest in the activity of writing unless you possess some feeling of futurity. The act of describing would involve some notion of the passage of time. Narrating would imply at least a hint of 'and then' and 'after that'. Any written or spoken sentence would naturally lean forward towards its development and conclusion, unlike my own paralysed time. Why should you even dream of explaining how, after an unexpected death, you might find yourself living in this profoundly altered temporal state? The risks of trying are clear enough: you'd resemble the survivor of the 1960s who bores everyone with tales of his inexpressibly memorable acid trips – then, as if worse were needed, you'd top it off with the layer of unassailable pathos due to your status as the mother of a dead child.

Nonetheless, however commonplace this condition of being 'outside time', when you're first in it, it's so quietly astonishing that you can't do other than take a cool interest in how you might characterize it. This, for several reasons. Because to concede at the outset that it's 'indescribable' would only isolate you further, when coming so close to your child's death is already quite solitary enough; because it's scarcely rare, for immeasurably vast numbers have known, and will continue to know, this sense of being removed from time, and so your efforts might well be familiar to everyone else who's also struggled to speak about this vivid state. Or perhaps it's also a kind of vanity, my hope that describing it might ring true for others who are in the same boat.

There's no specific noun for a parent of a dead child; nothing like the terms for other losses such as 'orphan' or 'widower'. No single word exists, either, for an 'adult child' – an awkward phrase which could suggest a large floppy-limbed doll. For such a historically common condition as outliving your own child, the vocabulary is curiously thin. The same phrases recur. For instance, many kindly onlookers will instinctively make use of this formula: 'I can't imagine what you are feeling.' There's a paradox in this remark, for it's an expression of sympathy, yet in the same breath it's a disavowal of the possibility of empathy. Undoubtedly it's very well meant, if (understandably) fear-filled. People's intentions are good; a respect for the severity of what they suppose you're enduring, and so a wish not to claim to grasp it. Still, I'd like them to *try* to imagine; it's not so difficult. Even if it's inevitable, or at any rate unsurprising, that those with dead children are regarded with concealed horror, they don't need to be further shepherded into the inhuman remote realms of the 'unimaginable'. So I want to try, however much against the odds, to convey only the one striking aspect: this curious sense of being pulled right outside of time, as if beached in a clear light.

My own instincts here happen to run in favour of de-dramatizing; but to properly de-dramatize, first you'd need to admit this strangeness fully into the compass of the discussable. Perhaps there may be at least a half-tellable ordinariness here. This demands witness. I'll offer some of that, if hesitantly, as I'd rather have steered clear of all autobiography. A few of my notes are reproduced below, though they can walk around only the rim of this experience. At times they loop back on themselves, for one effect of living inside such a temporal suspension is that your reflections will crop up all over again but as if, on each occasion, they're newly thought.

What follows is what I set down at the time at infrequent intervals, in the order that I lived it.

Two weeks after the death:

In these first days I see how rapidly the surface of the world, like a sheet of water that's briefly agitated, will close again silently and smoothly over a death. His, everyone's, mine. I see, as if I am myself dead. This perception makes me curiously light-hearted.

You share in the death of your child, in that you approach it so closely that you sense that a part of you, too, has died that instant. At the same time, you feel that the spirit of the child has leaped into you. So you are both partly dead and yet more alive. You are cut down, and yet you burn with life.

One month after the death:

This so-called 'work of grief' is turning out to be a shatteringly exhausting apprehension of the needed work of *living*. It demands to be fully lived, while the labour of living it is physically exhausting – like virulent jetlag, but surging up in waves.

The notes and emails of condolence have stopped arriving and I've acknowledged each of them. Yet after all this ritual and effort, he *still* hasn't come home. What more does he want?

So intricate and singular a living thing can't just vanish from the surface of life: that would run counter to all your accumulated experience. The day after his death, studiously wiping away what you realize are the last tangible traces: tiniest bits of his hair from the edge of the washbasin. This solid persistence of *things*. So then, the puzzle of what 'animation' is; of exactly what it is that's been crushed.

This instant enlargement of human sympathy. It's arrived in me at once. His death has put me in mind of those millions whose children were and are lost in natural disasters, starved, drowned, or systematically obliterated in wars; no wonder that bitterness and a loss of hope have filtered down the generations, with the resulting disengagement of those left alive. Millions disorientated, perhaps, by this quiet feeling of living, only just, on this near side of a cut between the living and the dead.

At the death of your child, you see how the edge of the living world gives onto burning whiteness. This edge is clean as a strip of guillotined celluloid film. First came the intact negative full of blackened life in shaded patches, then abruptly, this milkiness. This candid whiteness, where a life stopped. Nothing 'poetic', not the white radiance of eternity – but sheer non-being, which is brilliantly plain.

Five months after:

Apparently almost half a year has gone by since J disappeared, and it could be five minutes or half a century, I don't know which. There is so very little movement. At first I had to lie down flat for an hour each afternoon, because of feeling crushed as if by a leaden sheet, but by now I don't need to lie down. This slight physical change is my only intimation of time.

Knowing and also not knowing that he's dead. Or I 'know' it, but privately I can't feel it to be so. These fine gradations of admitting the brute facts of the case, while not feeling them; utterly different, though, from supposing that he's still alive somewhere else in this world. This isn't some ambiguity designed to blur the hard fact. Nor is it an imperfect anaesthetic.

This knowing and not knowing is useful, for it allows the truthful richness of all those shades of acknowledging and dissenting. Half-realizing while half-doubting, assenting while demurring, conceding while finding it ludicrously implausible – so many distinctions, all of them nicely in play. To characterize such accurate nuances as my 'denial' of his death would be off the mark. Yet who is policing my 'acceptance' of it?

What a finely vigorous thing a life is; all its delicate complexity abruptly vanished. Almost comical. A slapstick fall.

There's no relation, simply, between your recall of the courageously optimistic dead and your knowledge of the fall of sudden blackness. But you struggle to hold both in mind at once. You try to slot together the snippets of evidence – coffin, ashes, silent house, non-reappearance of child – to become fully convinced by the deduction that you have conscientiously drawn.

My head can't piece together the facts of a coffin under its roses and lilies, then the sifting gunmetal-grey ashes, with this puzzling absence of the enthusiastic person who left home to work abroad for a few days but has still not walked back in the door.

Not that I have *delusions*, as such. But a strong impression that I've been torn off, brittle as any dry autumn leaf, liable to be blown onto the tracks in the underground station, or to crumble as someone brushes by me in this public world where people rush about loudly, with their astonishing confidence. Each one of them a candidate for sudden death, and so helplessly vulnerable. If they do grasp that at any second their own lives might stop, they can't hold on to that expectation. As I do now. Later everyone on the street seems to rattle together like dead leaves in heaps.

Wandering around in an empty plain, as if an enormous drained landscape lying behind your eyes had turned itself outward. Or you find yourself camped on a threshold between inside and out. The slight contact of your senses with the outer world, your interior only thinly separated from it, like a membrane resonating on a verge between silence and noise. If it were to tear through, there's so little behind your skin that you would fall out towards the side of sheer exteriority. Far from taking refuge deeply inside yourself, there is no longer any inside, and you have become only outward. As a friend, who'd survived the suicide of the person closest to her, says: 'I was my two eyes set burning in my skull. Behind them there was only vacancy.'

I work to earth my heart.

Six months after:

A summer has gone, a cold autumn is setting in, but I've no sense of my time as having any duration, or any future. Time now is a plateau. I only know whether an event came before or after the date of the death. If there was a death. I didn't see the body. His body. Not that the sight always helps to anchor your belief in the fact. What a lumpish little word: 'dead'. And 'died' seems an increasingly silly verb. 'Dead', used of the lively J, strikes me as not only unlikely, but mistaken. A prematurely coarse verdict. Like John Donne's phrase; 'her death – which word wrongs her.'[1] Instead I want to say 'since he vanished'. That seems far more accurate. It's better conveyed in French or in Italian, where without any affectation you could call someone's death 'his disappearance', or you might naturally say that 'she has left us'.

Immediately J vanished, I fell into a solidarity with other bereaved parents: an imagined solidarity, because at that stage I didn't know any. I sought them out, online and in meetings and one-to-one, and I listen ardently to how they try to live on. So I can hear that everyone testifies to this wish once they're in the safe company of others in the same boat: the hope for their own rapid death. Yet I can't allow myself this comforting prospect, as I won't abandon my surviving children. Any more than I'll abandon the dead one. I never abandoned him in his life, and I've no intention of starting now, 'just because he's dead'. What kind of a reason would that be? I tried always to be there for him, solidly. And I shall continue to be. (The logic of this conviction: in order to 'be there', I too have died.)

A vicarious death. If a sheet of blackness fell on him, it has fallen on me too. As if I also know that blankness after his loss of consciousness.

This state is physically raw, and has nothing whatever to do with thinking sad thoughts or with 'mourning'. It thuds into you. Inexorable carnal knowledge.

The plainest simplest horror from which the mind flinches away: never to see that person again. The purely *cognitive* violence of it. Now you understand those ideas of the migration of spirits, or of reincarnation: to try to soften that blow. Or no, not to soften it – but to provide something for baffled cognition to grasp at.

I've decided that this slow head of mine has to be left alone to *not* manage to make its impossible deduction. Meanwhile I'll try to incorporate J's best qualities of easy friendliness, warmth, and stoicism, and I shall carry him on in that way. Which is the only kind of resurrection of the dead that I know about.

I am inching along. But not forward, or in any other decipherable direction. If it's crabwise, then it's without effective pincers. This deep tiredness, as if sharing his grave; although actually most of that dead boy was poured as fine charcoal powder straight into the sea.

Nine months after:

Now it's thirty-nine weeks, the duration of a pregnancy, since he vanished. As if a pregnancy had by now been wound backwards past the point of conception and away into its pre-existence.

What do the dead give us? A grip on the present instant in which we're now relentlessly inserted. Not in a contemplative sense, but vigorously. A carnal sensation. If to be dead is to exist outside of earthly time, then this tough-minded energetic 'living in the present' is also the life of the dead. My new ability to live in the present joins in that timelessness of being dead. Or the nearest I can get to it.

Ten months after:

This 'skewed' perception of time – isn't it perfectly to be expected? Nothing exceptionally distorted, but a common human experience which could be recognized through being described. How might you save the strangeness of this immobile non-time from being considered pathological; an evaluation which would further isolate its dwellers? But your democratizing impulse here can succeed all too well, as some hearers will comment briskly on your descriptive efforts, 'You mean, like the feeling of disturbed time you get after a bad break-up, or if you lose your job – well, surely that's a common experience.' And then, aside, 'She's becoming a real death bore,' they'll recoil, shaking their heads. Or so you fear. Is this the famous hypersensitivity of the bereaved at work in you?

No tenses any more. Among the recent labels for temporality is 'time dilation', referring to our perception's elasticity, its capacity to be baggy. But are there any neurological accounts of this feeling of completely arrested time? It feels as if some palpable cerebral alteration has taken place. As if, to make the obvious joke, your temporal lobes have been flooded and are now your a-temporal lobes.

I'll try again: a sudden death, for the one left behind, does such violence to the experienced 'flow' of time that it stops, and then slowly wells up into a large pool. Instead of the old line of forward time, now something like a globe holds you. You live inside a great circle with no rim. In the past, before J's idiotic disappearance, the future lay in front of me as if I could lean into it gently like a finger of land, a promontory feeling its way into the sea. But now I've no sense of any onward temporal opening, but stay lodged in the present, wandering over some vast saucer-like incline of land, some dreary wide plain like the banks of the river Lethe, I suppose. His sudden death has dropped like a guillotine blade to slice through my old expectation that my days would stream onwards into my coming life. Instead I continue to sense daily life as paper-thin. As it is. But this cut through any usual feeling of chronology leaves a great blankness ahead.

Now you expect another death – a remaining child's – to be announced to you at any moment, and you try to steady yourself for it. It's not so much fearfulness as a life poised in acute suspension. You're tensed for anything. No plans can be made for any future, so you must try to inhabit this present with equanimity and in good heart. This might sound like stoicism's programme. But it's no philosophical stance, nor is it valour that dictates your new approach to living; only your realization that now a familiar apprehension of passing time has been barred to you. Nothing, then, like the happier notion of 'seizing the day'. On the contrary: *there is no time to seize.* The former slim and orderly temporal line has been blown away, as if it had been reduced to ash as efficiently as your child's corpse.

'Only in the present moment is our happiness': the stoics' pronouncement. The irony is that now you've succeeded brilliantly in living exclusively in the present, but only as the result of that death. To endure, yes, but when the usual passage of time is in shards? What does your old philosophy of endurance mean, when there's no longer any temporality left in which to wait it out?

Impossible, caught in your sheltering space of no-time, to grasp that your child's dead when they stay so vividly present. As if they themselves haven't the least intention of lying down gracefully with folded hands.

Unanticipated death does such violence to your ordinary suppositions, as if the whole inductive faculty by which you'd previously lived has faltered. Its textbook illustration was always 'Will the sun rise tomorrow?' But now that induction itself is no more, the sun can't any longer be relied on to rise. And my son does not rise. This silly pun alone can reliably work its mechanical work.

For the first time you grasp that inhabiting the drift of time is a mutable perception; one which can stop, leaving you breathing but stranded, stock still. From this unexpected vantage point, you discover that the perception of a 'flowing' time must have been secreted by and then exuded from the mind, like a silkworm spinning out its silken thread from its jaws; but now its conditions of production, whatever they were, are destroyed. There's nothing of the intellect in this revelation. It stems entirely from visceral sensations.

You could try to describe this being outside time by using a string of negatives: you live in the breathlessness of sensing that everything might halt at the next heartbeat, you've no conviction that your small daily plans (which, comically, must still be made) will ever bear fruit – those negatives are true but unhelpful. For this state of a-temporality isn't experienced negatively. It is lucidly calm as it fills up your horizons. Though a novel element to you, it brings an unanxious and energetic simplicity. A crystalline life, concentrated in the instant, and pleased enough with it. This new time of yours may, in fact, be the time of the dead themselves.

Eleven months after:

At almost a year since he died – or he 'died', for the plain assertion of his death still sounds foolishly melodramatic – I read endless online papers in cardiac pathology. Eventually I try to stop my reading, then am overwhelmed by whirring 'what ifs': what if one of his doctors had noticed J's (in retrospect, blindingly evident) heart failure or had taken his fainting episodes seriously; what if I'd known to draw the right conclusions myself from the signs that I, living with him daily, could see; what if the proper diagnosis had been made, what the surgical options might have done, was it better for him to have died not knowing about his cardiomyopathy, or would he have wanted to have had more years, if impaired . . . All my furious study and speculation is the uselessness of thought trying to rewind time, to master what cannot be mastered. And *this* thought does nothing to stop it.

In your imagination, you will endlessly witness

the instant of your child's dying. But the accompanying struggle to realistically assess your degree of responsibility for the death needn't entail your 'masochism'. It seems vital to not flinch from the former, while not sliding into the latter. And to get that distinction clear, just for yourself, will demand a forensic labour. To take responsibility; the word means, to weigh things up. That testing the weight doesn't have to be a labour of guilt. Does it?

I had wanted un-frightened company. And yet I could sit alone, and needed to sit alone, to translate his autopsy report from its original Spanish with an online medical dictionary to hand, in a coolly determined rush of concentration. The living person was rather squeamish and he would not have cared for this. Needs must. I read on rapidly about the discovery of the corpse in a still-running bath, its good musculature (at that, he'd have brightened up), its chest cavity opened up by means of the conventional incision, the skull sawed so that the brain could be lifted out, the enlarged heart dissected on removal, the fluids in lungs and bladder inspected and measured.

The drive to know is cool-headed; this concentrated will to understand everything about your child's sudden death becomes intensely forensic, and dispassionate. Only much later would I wonder about, for instance, the degree of physical effort needed to shear open a chest. Or whether the ribs' cartilage is easily cut. This autopsy happened to be imperfect in settling for 'heart attack', as that conclusion did not fit its own findings of the enlarged heart which instead implied cardiomyopathy; and it demanded far more research into the nature of drowning, how you can distinguish death by water from death prior to immersion by the flooding of the lungs with small haemorrhaged flecks of blood. You read on rapidly, quietly through the pages, feeling yourself as expressionless as that chilled body on the pathologist's slab, which by now is so inert and drained of spirit for you that your difficult part lies elsewhere; in explaining later to others (though you'll spare them from hearing exactly what you've learned) why your work was necessary. That it wasn't some obsessed self-reproach, but that for the sake of your still-living children you'd needed to establish the true cause of their brother's death and its possible genetic implications for them. You don't want them to die too, through your avoidable ignorance. Many parents say this – that they will pursue the cause of death doggedly. Later I reflect that I had been too alone in my task. So that the local surgery could close my son's file, I take the translated autopsy report to a young GP, who glances at it, then sits with his head in his hands, saying, 'I wasn't trained to deal with this. We didn't get to read autopsies. This is absolutely horrendous.' Perhaps he doesn't yet have his own children. Or he does. I do my best to reassure him that it's usual to search out each detail, to try to know. To keep your child company in its death.

Maybe to stop grilling yourself about your remotest responsibility for the death would need some sense that a future and its customary logical furnishings were in place. But now they are not. All the usual supports for your reasoning, the unnoticed but vital connecting tissues of 'because' and 'then', have been severed. The old edifice of knowing now droops forward and flops without its scaffolding. So your uncertainties will return and return, as there's nothing to calm and secure them.

We can forgive ourselves for the death of our children.

Perhaps this forgiving ourselves will need to be done over and over again. I don't know.

Sixteen months after:

Superficially 'fine' as my daily air of cheerfulness carries me around with an unseen crater blown into my head, the truth is that my thoughts are turned constantly to life and to death; all that I can now attentively hold.

It still seems ludicrous to decide, finally, that I shall not see that face on this earth. What would be 'natural' would be his beaming reappearance, a bit sheepish at having been away from home for so long.

More limp puns abound: you conceived the child, but you can't conceive of its death.

The persisting impression of the living-on of the dead child as your mind ploughs on along its familiar cognitive furrows. It's like that cartoon image of Donald Duck running straight off the edge of a cliff, his webbed feet going on paddling wildly in the air – until he looks down. He'll only plummet once he's put together what he's just glimpsed, the ground far below, with his realization of his mid-air state.

Wherever can you find written accounts of this lived time without consequence? It's rare. Here, though, is Emily Dickinson's quatrain, relentlessly to the point:

> The thought behind I strove to join
> Unto the thought before,
> But sequence raveled out of sound
> Like balls upon a floor.

'Sequence raveled out of sound', indeed. One note no longer implies another's coming. You watch the water cascading from the tap to splash into the basin. Yet noting small events and their effects doesn't revive your former impression of moving inside time. The tap turns, water pours. You can observe sequence. Nothing, though, follows from this observation to propel you, too, onward into the old world of consequences.

Not that your sense of time is 'distorted'. What's changed is more radical than that. Simply, you are no longer *in* time. Only from your freshly removed perspective can you fully understand how our habitual intuitions of time are not without their limits, and can falter.

To tell someone with a dead child, 'You should move on,' is doubly thoughtless, because there's no medium left through which to move anywhere. We were drifting through our former time like underwater creatures furnished with gills that they didn't notice they had, until they were fished up out of their element and their breathing apparatus failed.

If there is ever to be any movement again, that moving will not be 'on'. It will be 'with'. With the carried-again child.

Your old stance is changed – not by melancholy, but by the shattering of that underlying intuition of moving in time, an intuition which you can't register until it's collapsed. If time was once flowing, extended, elongated – a river, a road, a ribbon – now the river is dammed, the road blocked, the ribbon slashed. Well-worn metaphors all shot to pieces.

He is not dead to me.

Two years after:

You live under the sign of the provisional. Often with faint amusement over little debates: do you unpack this coral dress from storage as if, when the summer arrives in a few months, you'll still be alive to wear it? Yes – but purely because you enjoy the zing of its colour today.

Two and a half years later:

Time arrested, as the triumph of metaphor, or so it would seem at first. Perhaps, though, it's more a crisscrossing and slippage of emotion, which you can only recount through descriptions which serve the dead and the living indiscriminately. So if this inability to grasp the fact of the death is my own lot, the dead themselves may well share it. All those many faiths in which the freshly and suddenly dead don't yet realize that they're dead, and so have to be placated, or to have novenas held for them, or their corpses sat up with, all night long, at wakes, now make perfect sense; those left behind need to keep a wary eye on their dead who can't be trusted not to reappear. And why wouldn't they be shocked and furious at being ousted from life?

Analogies ramify. Plunged in some florid jungle of 'as ifs', you sense them roaming everywhere, blossoming like bindweed, tying everything together then spiralling upward, entwining you and the dead in conjoined experience.

In how many ways this folded-together state appears. You already share the 'timeless time' of the dead child. As if you'd died too, or had lost the greater part of your own life. As if a new no-time stands still in your veins. That's the overarching 'as if'. Then there's an 'as if' of uttering, when the speech of the one left behind can turn staccato. That first day afterwards, speaking by phone to the funeral director, I needed to yet could not get the word 'ashes' out of my mouth without a strenuous physical struggle. 'Aa-aassh-aashhes,' came a dry stammer. As if uttered through sawdust. It wasn't any conscious repugnance at having to say that word only hours after my last glimpse of the living person. But something bodily felt. A cut fell between the thought and its voicing. My jaw must have worked over the word 'ashes' like that of a dying fish. Or it must have been as slack as

J's own mouth once the rigor mortis had worn off; but that analogy only comes to me now, well over two years later. Immediately after the death, my firm intention to speak the needed words 'disposal of his ashes' would not be carried out, physically. I'd believed that thought is made in the mouth, and is often discovered only through speaking aloud. Now on the contrary, to my own astonishment and embarrassment, my mouth was bluntly refusing to pronounce the phrase that waited clearly if silently voiced in my head. Previously I hadn't believed that speech is simply the translation of something already formulated in thought. Now I was faced with the evidence that sometimes it is, but that the translation can fail. No passage across the lips. The brain could calmly entertain the word. The mouth would not. 'Aaah-sssh . . .' it went. As if it had itself become sifted up thickly with ashes.

Whatever's the name for this transfer of affect? It's rather like that blurring of physical edges that happens between lovers: you become the other one, you can feel as if through their skin.

All this entangling with your dead child, though, becomes evident in thought only as you look back. At the time, you're naturally and easily inside several states. Or inside two lives. For if timelessness is the time of your dead, then you will go with them into their timelessness. Here you can live mundanely, indeed brightly. You're fused with the dead, as if to animate them. They draw you across to their side, while you incorporate them on your side.

Inside your sheltering thicket of branching 'as ifs', it's not only as if the ashes of your child had blocked your own mouth, but as if your own future is as neatly guillotined; as if you wipe away the physical traces of the dead as cleanly as that life itself was wiped away; as if in the same breath as the flow of time halts, your old sense of your innerness drops into pure exteriority; as if these are sensations of being with our dead while they can no longer sense time nor have any interior sense of themselves; as if, yet without actually believing this, you'll be with the dead when you die; as if now both of you inhabit a companionate exile rather than being two parallel units of loneliness; as if, as you'd carried the unborn child inside you, so again you carry its lively memory; as if you need to die yourself to continue that long habit of attentiveness which can't immediately be resiled from the dead. As if care will not give up its affectionate task.

Later, I'm struck by the force of so much being with the dead. I hear it constantly in other mothers of dead children. Such imagined empathy seals your sense of stopped time. Like one of those dogged pursuers in classical mythology, you've followed your dead into the underworld, one foot in either realm like Orpheus turning back on the threshold to check that Eurydice was still following behind him, almost safely retrieved. If your feeling of arrested time were indeed the time shared with your dead, then your unwanted re-entry to the usual flow of the world's time would mean that, like poor Orpheus, you'd come back alone. Is the force of this story that we can only stay in the company of our dead for as long as we don't *notice* them as really separate from us, caught in their different realm? Although that fierce Demeter contrived a better deal: to fetch her daughter Persephone back from Pluto's darkness for half of each year at a time. Shared custody.

These skeins of 'as ifs' don't arrive as considered comparisons, though, but as direct feelings. In fact 'as if' scarcely applies here, although you're forced to use it in retrospect to try to convey this many-layered impression. Something more intimate's in play than straightforward analogy. Yet it's also something removed from any direct 'identification'. It's neither your sameness with your dead, nor your full separateness from them. And I'd fight shy of considering it magic to fight off the fact of the death. It's not fanciful bewitchment. It feels fleshly, and solidly true to this fresh world of feeling. Once you can no longer experience any flow of time, any sequence, or any induction, then sensations that once would have been incommensurable can now flourish side by side. What then do we call this multiplied perception? Liminal?

Not only will 'as ifs' flourish, but also the more familiar and expected 'what ifs', whose prickings, like showers of arrows, torment those in the aftermath of a sudden death. They position you imaginatively before it happened, so that now you're in a position to have prevented it.

How tactful we become in avoiding all and any expressed measurements of loss. Never would I compare my state with that of, say, a widow's. Never would I lay claim to 'the worst grief of all'. And, among my own kind, never would I compare my own infinitely lighter lot with that of the parent of a murdered or a tortured child, or a suicidal child, or one killed in a stupid accident, or one very young, dying painfully slowly.

Still, you needn't have erected some dubious hierarchy of grief in order to wonder what's particular to losing a child, of any age, and why this loss feels so different in kind from your experience of other deaths. And this question demands more than the obvious observation that the stronger the love for the dead, the sharper the loss. Perhaps what's specific is this: that with the death of your child, your own experience of time may be especially prone to disturbance because the lost life had, so to speak, previously unfurled itself inside your own life.

If you had once sensed the time of your child as quietly uncoiling inside your own, then when that child is cut away by its death, your doubled inner time is also 'untimely ripped'. Yours, and the child's. The severance of the child's life makes a cut through your own. You as its mother can no longer be present to yourself in the old temporal way. A sculptural imagination rises to grip you; the hollow of the old shelter for the living child has now been gouged out of you. It was the space of the child's past, which used to lie like an inner shell enveloped by your own time. That child you had, alone, when you were young yourself, a child you grew up with, nested like a Russian doll whose shorter years sat within yours, gave you a time that was always layered. Then you held times, in the plural.

Yet after this scooping-out by the death, a fresh incorporation arrives: the child gets reanimated in your effort to embody its qualities and carry them onwards. Perhaps this is the peculiar fate of mothers of dead children: still to contain that other life, and to shelter it twice over. Once before the child's birth, and once after the death when you're left with an impression of a spirit internalized. This partial rebirth can be exhaustingly preoccupying; much like a pregnancy run in reverse, spooling back from the point of the child's death to its incorporated life in you. And this exerts itself in the pressure of your forceful but not especially disconcerting sensation of living outside time.

I dread forgetting his odd blend of being quietly wry and yet completely without guile. My mind figures, 'Well, if J hasn't called me for such an unprecedentedly long time, then maybe it's true after all that he died.' Then I'm embarrassed but amused to overhear this silly calculus totting itself up in me.

Whenever I need to mention to someone that 'my son died', it still sounds to me like a self-dramatizing lie. Tasteless. Or it's an act of disloyalty to him. For I don't experience him as in the least dead, but simply as 'away'. Even if he'll be away for my remaining lifetime. My best hope's to have a hallucination of his presence when I'm dying myself.

Perhaps only through forgetting the dead could it become possible to allow them to become dead. To finally *be* dead. And that could only follow – once time itself had taken the initiative here – from consigning them to a time that had decided to resume its old flow. Of its own accord. When or if this may ever happen, I can't know. And can't want it.

Time 'is' the person. You're soaked through with it. This enormous lurch into arrested time isn't some philosophical brooding about life's fragility. It's not the same 'I' who lives in her altered sense of no-time, but a reshaped person. And I don't know how she'll turn out. If writing had once been a modest work of shaping and correcting, now all your small mastery has been smashed by the fact of your child's death. *That* you can't edit.

You find yourself noting this, but without ever

needing or even wanting to have recourse to words like *sorrow*, *grief*, *mourning*. As if all those are too familiar, too sepia, and almost decorative, blandly containing. You entertain no reflections, either, that a life will leave its reverberations hanging in the air like a passage of music – nothing so sweetly melancholic. Instead, your living in this instant, this thinnest imaginable sliver of being, turns out to be hard-edged. Side views are occluded without any softening penumbra. Your sight is pared down like tunnel vision. Yet to your narrowed focus, the dead of this entire city are present all at once, elbowing in the streets. Silhouettes stream everywhere: horses, carriages, cars. Traffic ghosts smash right through you whenever you cross a road. Grey ribbons of painless collisions. But these aren't misty or violet-tinted, are nothing to do with 'mourning' as you might once have fancied it. This is sharp and harshly clear. Your surrounding fluid of intuitive time had abruptly drained away. Now you live in an unshaded clarity of dry air. Its translucent simplicity buoys you up.

By what means are we ever to become re-attached to the world?

Two years and ten months later:

No time at all. No time.

Three years after:

And by now I've stopped making these notes.

What follows is a postscript, drawing on them, about what I've had to learn about living in arrested time.

Postscript

What can we do with such solitary experiences of violently new and hitherto unsuspected states of temporal perception; what sense can we try to make of them? To show what I mean about 'time lived but without its flow', I'd have needed to do yet more reporting on the visceral state of being thrown outside time for a period of years. That state may sound unreal, implausible. Our customary intuitions of time strongly suggest that it would be both perceptually impossible and practically unliveable. Yet it's surely a state that's common enough, and is indeed manageable. Inside their senses of arrested time, millions must live today, and have lived. The deaths of their children are apt to induce profound dislocation in the experienced time of those left alive. They are thrown into 'timeless time'. However, despite the fact that such human losses occur constantly, this ensuing state of a-temporality seems largely to escape recorded notice.

For to outlive a sudden death makes it evident that your ordinary time, which had once 'flowed', had never been much like a clear stream, or a fluid held in glass. That old kind of lived time was no simple medium, and nothing finely transcendent. It had always been thick. It must have been another aspect of 'the flesh of the world'; active, changeable, and formative.[2] Now, though, your distinct sensation of a newly halted time – or rather, of a non-time – has blown away that unremarked thickness, and instead has dropped you down in its own still landscape of brilliant clarity. Perhaps yours might be cited as a version of akinetopsia, that rare condition in which you mislay your perception of motion, like the patient who found pouring a cup of tea difficult 'because the fluid appeared to be frozen, like a glacier'.[3] Nevertheless you find that you survive perfectly well in this new non-time of sheer stasis. Rather than being just a temporal swerve, it's more of a stepping-outside the entire sheltering sky of temporality itself – into a not unpleasant state of tremendous simplicity, of easy candour and bright emptiness.

You've slipped into a state of a-chronicity. From its serene perspective you realize, to your astonishment, that to dwell inside a time that had the property of 'flowing' was merely one of a range of possible temporal perceptions. For your time can pause, and you with it – though you're left sharply alive within its stopping. Your apprehension of sequence itself is halted. Where you have no impression of any succession of events, there is no linkage between them, and no cause. Anything at all might follow on from any one instant. You are tensed for anything – or, equally, are poised for nothing. No plans can be entertained seriously, although you keep up an outward show of doing so. Where induction itself has failed, so does your capacity for confident anticipation. So your task now is to inhabit the only place left to you – the present instant – with equanimity, and in as much good heart as you can contrive. For one moment will not, now, carry you onward to the next.

This vivid new sensation of a-temporality differs from some more readily comprehended 'distorting' of time, for it has no traces of the old familiar temporal shapes, and it resists intelligible description. Sharply different, it's a physical perception. Not a reflective state of mind, or an act of introspection leaning on an exhausted figure of speech, but a perception as bodily immediate, as inescapable, as a feeling of thirst. The irony is that this strong experience resurrects the life in the dead metaphor of 'time stopped' – while the occasion for this linguistic reanimation, the formerly living child, stays stubbornly dead.

*

Still, I find myself wanting to claim time's standstill as an ordinary enough phenomenon – if not inevitable, then perfectly to be expected in the wake of a sudden death. As a condition not to be quickly categorized as 'pathological' and then consigned to an isolating silence, but rather to be recognized as common enough and capable of being openly discussed. How, then, can I struggle to convey this distinctive experience of living inside a new nontime – while in the same breath I want to save it from being treated as unapproachable, and exceptional? That, straightforwardly enough, might be a matter of allowing the myriad specificities of different losses their differing temporal impacts. A chronic or a terminal illness, for example, may force on its sufferer a vehemently transformed kind of time. That will possess its own particular charge, not to be flattened into a false equivalence with other kinds of changed temporalities.

Occasioned by the unexpected death, your enormous shift away from your old grasp of time is far removed from your predictable meditations on the fragility of life, from your wistful philosophizing, or from your crushed expectations. Your altered temporality is not to do with any kind of *taking thought*. It is prior to that, and supremely indifferent to lament and to cogitation alike. Instead it feels foundational: to do with a change in the entire structure of cognition. An unanticipated and irrevocable vanishing smashes through your habitual cognitive assumption that objects and people will continue to exist, to reappear. The person who says, 'I keep expecting to hear his key in the door any moment,' isn't merely falling back on a well-worn trope. She's issuing a factual report. Once so ferociously shaken up, cognition can't readily regroup its forces to reassemble with its old anticipation intact. The entire stance inside which you'd previously lived is changed. Not by any disfiguring melancholia on your part, or even by simple reflective sadness – but by an upheaval of that pre-conscious topography through which your old apprehension of the world had once quietly moved. So those who lose a child will go out with the lost one into their timelessness. Into 'timeless time'. This experience, as I reflected, must be the time of the dead. Or it's as near as you can get to entering into that time, or that non-time.

'So to speak' comes the quick qualification here. Your own changed perception of time, so hard to describe aloud convincingly, is echoed in the stumbling ordinary language about the being of the dead. The very grammar of discussing a death falters in its conviction – in the same breath that the focus of talk, the formerly living person, himself disintegrates. Even the plainest 'He died' is a strange sentence, since there's no longer a human subject to sustain that 'he'. And what of the phrase 'his body', once there's no surviving 'he' to animate it? Lydia Davis has a lovely piece on this, a darkly light and plaintive speculation that she calls 'Grammar Questions':

> When he is dead, everything to do with him will be in the past tense. Or rather, the sentence "He is dead" will be in the present tense, and also questions such as "Where are they taking him?" or "Where is he now?"
>
> But then I won't know if the words *he* and *him* are correct, in the present tense. Is he, once he is dead, still "he", and if so, for how long is he still "he"?[4]

It's as if any death causes the collapse of the simplest referring syntax. As if the grammatical subject of the sentence and the human subject have been felled together by the one blow. Yet at the same time, the continuing possibilities for discussing the no longer existing person induce a curious linguistic quasi-resurrection.[5] Perhaps language, at least, possesses a belief in spirit. No wonder that the puzzles of lost animation, and reanimation, become a driving preoccupation for those left alive. Those gibbering souls of Orphic myth might suggest that the scattering of the *anima* is also a syntactical taking flight, while even the most secular mind may find it hard to conceive of a death without a continuation, some variant of a released soul. And this has its linguistic reasons. No subject can easily be conceived as extinguished, because language itself doesn't want to allow that thought; its trajectory is always to lean forward into life, to push it along, to propel the dead onward among the living.

Such daily curios of expression as 'she's died' are readily shuffled along with. They're pragmatic. Far more linguistically intractable, though, is the effort to show the condition of stopped time. Again you'll try to convey your discovery that everyday acts of telling and describing assume the speaker's aware-ness of passing time with each use of an implicit 'next'. But once there's no longer any element of sequence, because that usual intuition of flowing time has been halted, narration itself can't proceed. Any attempt at descriptive writing soon reaches an impasse, for it could normally have relied, tacitly, on its own unfolding. Not so now. A life of no time can't be recounted. Your very condition militates against narrative.

Maybe only the cinema could show it. Not by means of any cinematic plot, certainly, but through the camerawork itself.[6] Still, here we are on the printed page, with what there is to hand.

*

Looping around, I repeat myself, yet am compelled to keep trying to say it: to live on after a death, yet to live without inhabiting any temporal tense yourself, presents you with serious problems of what's describable. This may explain the paucity of accounts of arrested time. To struggle to narrate becomes not only an unenticing prospect, but structurally impossible. Not because, as other people might reasonably assume, you are 'too shocked' to wish to write a word, or because you are 'in denial' – but because, as the movement of time halts for you, so do all those customary 'befores' and 'afters' that underpin narration. A sentence slopes forward into its own future, as had your former intuition of a mobile time. But now your newly stopped time is stripped of that direction. Or rather, the whole notion of directedness has gone.

It was only when a familiar intuition of sequence eventually and spontaneously restored itself, having 'taken its time' over the passage of about three years, that I could begin to sort out my fragmented notes, and to start on these paragraphs.

*

While many philosophies of time have argued, for instance, over how atomized instants of perception may be felt as a unified streaming, this other feeling of 'timelessness' seems not to be mentioned. This lacuna must be due to the fact that the *experience* of a-temporality systematically undercuts its own articulation. Here it can't speak itself, because the usual articulations of syntax, in its continuities, are snapped. Perhaps this is why so very little seems to have been published about the effects of a child's sudden death on the experienced time of those left living.[7] While through the usual memorial outlets, most published expressions of sentiment tend to be highly convention-bound. Neither this descriptive silence nor this sweetened overlay is surprising, if you think of the impassable structural barriers to telling. When, thrown into your freshly timeless condition, you can no longer have the least anticipation of your own future or take any interest in it, so implausible does its arrival seem, your usual language of narrating is curtailed in the same blow. Your very *will to tell* your violently novel state of timelessness is sapped, because you sense that your most determined efforts can't reach others; you come to feel that syntax itself is set against you here, because it must rely on conventional temporality to function at all.

If your time as a child had once thrown you into language, now you discover that narrative language had sustained you across time. Its 'thens' and 'nexts' had once unfolded themselves placidly. But now that time has abruptly gone away from you, your language of telling has left with it. For now an unsuspected scenario has enfolded you in its blinding illumination. You *are* time. You are saturated with it, rather than standing apart from it as a previously completed being who was free to move in it.[8] In your old unremarked inclination towards the future, there was something that had also shaped your apprehension of yourself. As in Merleau-Ponty's observation, 'It is of the essence of time to be not only actual time, or time which flows, but also time which is aware of itself, for the explosion or dehiscence of the present towards a future is the archetype of *the relationship of self to self*, and it traces out an interiority or an ipseity'.[9] So it would follow that both time and your own being, in their mutual implication, had formerly leant out and forward to the world. Your interior 'revelation of self to self' was also 'the hollow in which time is formed.'[10]

Then – to follow the spirit and the logic of these reflections – whatever happens once you're thrown entirely outside of time's motion and you find yourself abruptly divorced from this mutual implication? Do you now say that *you* have stopped? Admittedly something still goes on; you walk about, you sleep a bit, you do your best to work, you get older. Yet in essence you *have* stopped. You're held in a crystalline suspension. Your impression of your own interiority has utterly drained away, and you are pure skin stretched tightly out over vacancy. You abide.[11]

Nevertheless your search for any evidence of fellow feeling is restless, almost comically so. You're paralysed and not, as far as you know, temporarily (for this condition feels eternal) but temporally. And yet some longing drives you onward to comb through any writing that might carry the reassurance that this cessation of your time is both well known and fully recorded. At times of great tension, we may well find ourselves hunting for some published resonances in literature of what we've come to feel. I realize that this might quickly be condemned as a sentimental search for 'identification', for the cosiness of finding one's own situation mirrored in print. Still, I think we can save it from that withering assessment. Instead we might reconsider the possibility of a literature of consolation, what that could be or what it might do.

Wherever is the literature – for it *must* exist, it's needed – that deals closely with this strange arresting of time? Certainly there's a seventeenth-century poetry of temporal distortion. Impossible, here, to embark on a survey. But to light on just one fine example, the elegist Henry King writes of how, after his young wife's death, his time slowed and its sequences went into reverse.

> […] For thee, loved clay,
> I languish out, not live, the day,
> Using no other exercise
> But what I practise with mine eyes;
> By which wet glasses I find out
> How lazily time creeps about
> To one that mourns; this, only this,
> My exercise and business is.
> So I compute the weary hours
> With sighs dissolved into showers.
> Nor wonder if my time go thus
> Backward and most preposterous.[12]

However, this much we have heard of, or we already know as the sad distortion of the mourner's time. Whereas Wordsworth's heavily analysed quatrains of 1798 seem in their very construction to enact that temporal fall from mobility into stillness:

> A slumber did my spirit seal;
> I had no human fears:
> She seemed a thing that could not feel
> The touch of earthly years.
>
> No motion has she now, no force:
> She neither hears nor sees,
> Rolled round in earth's diurnal course
> With rocks and stones and trees.

Between these two stanzas, there's a silent heavy crash of altered time. Now the natural historical past has snapped into a timeless present tense. And the second stanza also happens to carry the feeling of the one who lives on, but as if also lacking motion and force, in an uninflected present.

I'll leap on like a grasshopper in search of a rare but steadying blade of grass: for the radical stasis of time, one decisive note is Emily Dickinson's, in about 1864. This had first struck me in my notes above. Here's the piece in full:

> I felt a cleaving in my mind
> As if my brain had split;
> I tried to match it, seam by seam,
> But could not make them fit.
>
> The thought behind I strove to join
> Unto the thought before,
> But sequence raveled out of sound
> Like balls upon a floor.[13]

An earlier version of this poem had the line 'But sequence raveled out of reach'. The initial choice of 'reach' was easier and more obvious than the intense resonances of the noun 'sound' on which Emily Dickinson finally settled. (She didn't need to use 'sound' for the purposes of rhyming, since it falls at the end of a line that's structurally unrhymed within the quatrain. So 'sound' was her unconstrained revision, picked purely for its meaning.) Her eventual adoption of 'sequence raveled out of sound' implies that sound is the natural ally or shelter of the sequential or consecutive. There's an obvious association of sounds and sequences; with a passage of music or simply a scale, one note implies the coming of a next.[14] A first sound will lean towards a second sound, anticipating and promising it, even if to say so relies on retrospect. Even the harshest concatenation of discordant notes is still a sequence, in the sense of a succession pulled together on the ear.

But in Dickinson's poem her 'sequence' has been abstracted, so that now it is standing as a noun, a thing. And this new thing has scrambled itself clean away from sound, has gone shooting off across the floor like dropped balls of knitting wool. So far so good: sound, embodied as a vessel that would usually hold sequence, is divorced from it.

Yet without making unduly heavy weather of Emily Dickinson's eventual selection of this counter-intuitive 'sound', we could reflect a bit further. Sound is sustained on the ear by its repetition, and by the expectation that another sound will follow on. But now we hear that 'Sequence raveled out of sound'. What, though, would sound itself become, if the possibility of succession were to abandon it? This wholesale scrambling or 'raveling' of sequence in Dickinson's poem seems to imply something radical for *temporal* as well as for aural cognition. If sequence were truly to fall apart from sound, then the hearer could no longer expect any future unrolling, or could discern any principle of successive sounding. Each element of sound and sequence would, through this split, be rendered unintelligible in and by its new separateness. And their dissociation would sever our whole intuition of normally experienced time, which relies on extension, anticipation, and consequence. The separation of sound from sequence would chip away at consecutive thinking, and so at the whole principle of induction. And this is exactly what can happen in the aftermath of a sudden death. Or at least I found it to be so.

Dickinson's poem asserts that an associative chain may snap and scatter all its elements. If, in conjunction with this, we take Hegel's idea of sound as apt to grip and secure you by means of its sequences of notes, then such a break in continuity could bring about a corresponding change to your being. (Which indeed is what you sense happening, once you arrive in stopped time.) If, as he proposes, your perceptions of a train of vanishing sounds are germane to your self-sensing, then a disruption of your grasp of their sequence would alter your own presence to yourself. Again, this is what can happen in the wake of a sudden death. No longer are you unconsciously sustained by that pulsating instant-upon-instant intuition of yourself in time, which buoys you up; and which does so, even as each successive tick of the present will naturally obliterate the preceding one.

The self itself, declares Hegel, belongs to time, and coincides with time as it moves to and fro between its self-immediacy and its self-separation. Time *is* the being of the self. So much so that sound's own time, including its vanishing succession of myriad instants, 'sets the self in motion'.[15] You are, in effect, founded and sustained in the sequence of rhythm. So to be abruptly inside the experience of a-temporality, which must be without any sounding rhythm and without any confident expectation of futurity, would mean that you lived a kind of prolonged suspension. That condition is what's being shown in Emily

Dickinson's poem as 'sequence raveled out of sound' – and discovering her taut description comes as a relief.

Could we find anything more to consider about the possibility of a 'literature of consolation' – or is that almost a repugnant thought? Perhaps it's a question of a way of starting again, but a recommencing which doesn't entail an imagined restoration or a smoothing-over of what is lost. When someone close to you has died suddenly and unexpectedly, it's likely that at least one benign person will tell you to re-read Freud's 'Mourning and Melancholia'. But less prescriptive, and more sympathetic, than that essay is the older Freud's remark in his letter to a friend, written after the death of his daughter Sophie: 'Although we know that after such a loss the acute state of mourning will subside, we also know we shall remain inconsolable and will never find a substitute, no matter what may fill the gap; even if it be filled completely, it nevertheless remains something else. And actually this is how it should be [. . .] it is the only way of perpetuating that love which we do not want to relinquish.'[16]

So the gap will still remain detectable. It hangs on, as 'something else'. It's noticeable precisely *as* a filled gap, where the act of replacing keeps prominent. Which is as good as it gets. Here I'll make what may sound like a strange leap – to suggest that the same kind of 'preservation through replacement' happens in rhymed or metrical verse, and its paused and then resumed internal time: you stop, you repeat, you continue, you repeat but differently, you stop, you go ahead. Much like a version of Samuel Beckett's 'I can't go on, I'll go on'. Or his 'something is taking its course'. But a variant: 'something is being carried on'. The familiar but then the differing, in the next breath. Which is exactly what happens both in rhyme, and in your own gradual 'reanimation', so to speak, after you've been very near to a death. Nothing has changed, and yet it all has. You are returned after your brush with another's death, a brush that seemed to have stopped you, too – and you've been returned differently. You return, knowing more.

It's true to the nature of a return, including your own return from your proximity to another's death, that often it won't be an arrival at the same place.

And you yourself will not be the same. But something, nevertheless, stays: recognition as *re*-cognition; to know again, but because of the interval, to know a bit differently. Not through a replacement or a restoration of the lost object or word, for any new rhyme must embody a slight shift yet preserve the trace of the original, holding an outline of a gap that, even after it has been 'filled in', remains in a listening ear. Rhyme and rhythm keep their forms in, and through, echo's work; this reiterating sonic alteration isn't any melancholic shortcoming but part of the architecture of the poem. Like Freud's letter: 'no matter what may fill the gap; even if it be filled completely, it nevertheless remains something else. And actually this is how it should be.'

A poem may well be carried by oscillation, a to-and-fro, rather than by some forward-leaning chronological drive. It both sanctions and enacts an experience of time which is not linear. And your own time, in the immediate wake of someone's unexpected death, isn't linear. That might sound like a capricious comparison – between the workings of rhyme, and living through another's death, where you were very close to that person. Where you loved that person. But my guess is that rhyme may do its minute work of holding time together; making a chain of varied sound-stitches across time, a link to represent that feeling of sequence which may have been lost when the writer's or reader's usual temporal 'flow' has been cut by another's abrupt death.

Yet the sheer contingency of what in any particular language rhymes with what is never far away. There's an obvious impersonality about rhyme (its sound resemblances aren't resemblances of meaning – or not habitually); while rhyme, as well as rhythm, is in the same breath deeply personal in its indwelling in the mind's ear. Like a marriage of the material and the ideal. Of the stuff of words and their thought. It's a happy and a curious accident of the English language that the word 'rhyme' does itself rhyme with the word 'time'. And indeed, that both of these rhyme with 'chime', which itself means – a sounding repetition. Time suffers severance and is potentially joined again by rhyme. But I'm not claiming a 'therapeutics' or a curative aspect for rhyme. It can't mend the split between the usual forward movement of time and its stasis in the person caught at a standstill. Although memorial poems which are both strongly metrical and rhymed are what people seem 'instinctively' to turn to when in search of what to read at a funeral, there's scarcely consolation for loss in a formally structured poem. Still, such a poem may, to use an old-fashioned word, work as an emblem. A sounding emblem.

Emblematic of what? Of a loss at the moment when it's imperceptibly starting to shift; of the fact that there is change – you have been changed yourself, by your proximity to the death of an intimate – but also a return. This return is not to the same. As a rhyme is close but not identical, not an immaculate substitution but a recollection, while its sounding anticipates what's to come. This pulsating alteration-in-recognition comes close to the experience of a stopped time which is now unobtrusively, hesitantly – even reluctantly – finding a first breath of its future.

In contemporary fiction, a state of changed cognition after an unexpected death, and a porous sense of your own edges, is – to my limited knowledge – rarely shown. But Don DeLillo, in his 2001 novel *The Body Artist*, offers a kind of ghost, an unsettled and unsettling male presence who seems to speak from some a-temporal realm. He is, in effect, an occasional mouthpiece for the heroine's newly dead husband. She reflects on the condition of this disquieting visitor in her house:

> Time is supposed to pass, she thought. But maybe he is living in another state. It is a kind of time that is simply and overwhelmingly there, laid out, un-occurring, and he lacks the inborn ability to receive this condition. What ability? There is nothing he can do to imagine time existing in reassuring sequence, passing, flowing, happening – the world happens, it has to, we feel it – with names and dates and distinctions. His future is unnamed. It is simultaneous, somehow, with the present. Neither happens before or after the other and they are equally accessible, perhaps, if only in his mind.[17]

This passage is an extraordinarily precise account of the feeling of a life that continues, but does so outside any perceived changing time. DeLillo's suddenly widowed heroine, too, appears to have suffered an altered temporal sense of her own, since eventually – and what she reports here recalls Hegel's meditations – she comes to want to find again 'the flow of time in her body, to tell her who she was'.[18]

Yet this unpredictable point of your re-entry to a communicable social life and its familiar chronology will usher in its own great sadness. If it's your 'restoration' to the usual world, it's certainly not a restoration that you can celebrate. The cost of recovering your conventional apprehension of flowing time is intolerably high. The dead slip away, as we realize that we have unwillingly left them behind us in their timelessness. Much like Eurydice, who slid back from Orpheus' grasp just as he was on the threshold of re-entering the upper world with her. You would not have wanted this second, now final, loss. (Still, your own *wanting* is neither here nor there; you have also learnt this.)

Some part of you may still remain in the underworld, so to speak. The loss of your child continues to undo the separate singularity of your body and to refashion your sense of its edges. Not as a female biology of cyclical repetition, but a very different phenomenon. This isn't at all cyclical, and it's not felt as purely interior to the singular body. Rather, it's a historical time; the times of the child are contained and sheltered within your own. Fanny Howe's poem has voiced the start of this process as a temporal-spatial disruption:

> Each thing is sewn into time, then
> Having a child
> Is the most extreme caprice
> A smashing of space [19]

Yet whether they envisage a doubled containing, or a crashing through the neatness of an earlier time into a new dimension, all such reflections raise some tentative notion of a 'maternal temporality'. But could that be entertained in a way that wouldn't sink it into an all-engulfing and bodily-based maternalism? Arguably there's an understanding of the idea of a maternal temporality that wouldn't make such grandiose universal claims, but instead would spring from a particular affective history. In effect, it's a temporality of love – if the affection between the living and the now dead had been strong enough.

(Or it might even be a temporality of hate – while we might assume that a history of indifference would leave little mark.)

This affective history will extend your usual scope of felt time well beyond your own skin. In the past you had sensed your living child's time, including the physically interior time of its gestation as well as its early growing and independent life, as if it were internal to your own. You had aged in tandem with it. But now the time of the vanished child has been cut away from your impression of your interior time. As I'd noted, it's as if, from a set of nested Russian wooden dolls, the innermost ones had fallen out.

Emily Dickinson described as a state of 'dear retrospect' that act of looking back over the course of another's extinguished life, as if you shared it. This retrospect may well occur acutely after a child's death. For your purchase on your own lifetime would always have included that child's time as well as yours, however brief or however long its life. After its sudden disappearance, your temporal intuition becomes violently altered by the scooping away of that doubled sense of time that you'd lived in before, if without always being aware of it. Yet in this same moment of subtraction, the dead one, although now sheared away from your old conjoined temporality, now comes to re-inhabit your newly arrested time vividly, as an incorporated presence. In a shared a-temporality.

Although you're now turned intently toward the death, as you must be, your sentiments are not remotely melancholic. In your new perception of time, there's this fresh kind of 'carrying forward'. Your previous history has been reshaped, as your being in time has now become demarcated differently yet again. Its boundaries are extended by and then after the death, as they had once been by and then after the birth. Half bitten away by the child's disappearance, your time is nevertheless augmented – for the time of the dead is, from now on, freshly contained within your own.

How to think historically about all those myriad lived temporalities that find themselves increasingly resonant and densely layered, precisely because they've come to include the times of others? Any nominally single life, be it female or male, may in practice be thickened with the work of carrying and preserving the times of its dead, while it may also be holding the times of its still-living children. Such generational temporalities may sustain – or may erode – their bearers. As these several temporalities are intermingled within each person, they'll also run across and between people, so to speak, and they will become transpersonal. Multiplied, they can extend their legacies of apathy or of tranquil resignation; of despair or of furious energy; of bitterness or of a withdrawn indifference to the public world.

All this whirring on the page in the name of taking thought – and still the stubborn dead don't return to put it straight. A suggestion, then, in response to the question of what may characterize the experience of a time suspended, but nevertheless lived, after the death of a child: perhaps it's just this elaborate, dynamic, silent temporal abundance, even as this is also an abundance in loss. For such a maternal temporality owns its distinctive kinds of erosion, containment, paralysis, and augmentation in its overlapping of the living with the living, and of the living with the dead.

ACKNOWLEDGEMENTS

This essay was initially published by Capsule Editions, London, in 2012, and I'm very grateful to its editors, Edmund Hardy and James Wilkes, for supporting its first appearance.

I am thankful to Picador, and especially to Kish Widyaratna for her invaluable help.

Max Porter's introduction is generous beyond words; I thank him wholeheartedly for it.

ENDNOTES

1   In his 'A Nocturnal upon St Lucy's Day', c.1627.
2   Maurice Merleau-Ponty, *The Visible and the Invisible* (Evanston, IL: Northwestern University Press, 1968), pp. 130–55.
3   J. Zihl, D. von Cramon, and N. Mai, 'Selective disturbance of movement vision after bilateral brain damage', *Brain*, 106 (1983), pp. 313–40.
4   Lydia Davis, 'Grammar Questions' in *Varieties of Disturbance* (New York: Farrar, Straus and Giroux, 2007) and in *The Collected Stories of Lydia Davis* (New York: Farrar, Straus and Giroux, 2009), pp. 527–9.
5   As debated by Bertrand Russell's 1905 'theory of descriptions', in which a bald King of France stars.
6   As in Lucrecia Martel's 2008 film *The Headless Woman*, which includes shots inside the shut windows of a car, or in the 1960s and onwards, those very prolonged and steady panning takes in Straub–Huillet movies.
7   But see the work of Lenore C. Terr on children's time perception, including her paper 'Time and Trauma', *Psychoanalytic Study of the Child*, 39 (1984), pp. 633–65.

8   See Merleau-Ponty: 'To analyze time is not to follow out the consequences of a pre-established conception of subjectivity, it is to gain access, through time, to its concrete structure.' *Phenomenology of Perception* (London: Routledge & Kegan Paul, 1962), p. 410.

9   Merleau-Ponty, *Phenomenology of Perception*, p. 426.

10 Ibid., p. 431.

11 Merleau-Ponty, again citing Heidegger, adds: 'I am myself time, a time which "abides" and does not flow or change, which is what Kant says in various places.' *Phenomenology of Perception*, p. 421.

12 Henry King, 'The Exequy', in *Poems, Elegies, Paradoxes and Sonnets* (London: J. G. for Richard Marriot, 1657).

13 Emily Dickinson, *The Complete Poems of Emily Dickinson.* Boston: Little, Brown, 1924; Bartleby.com, 2000. www.bartleby.com/113/. [29/01/2019].

14 Helen Vendler comments on this in her *Dickinson: Selected Poems and Commentaries* (Cambridge, MA: Harvard University Press, 2010), pp. 358–9.

15 G. W. F. Hegel, *Hegel's Aesthetics*, trans. by T. M. Knox, 2 vols. (Oxford: Clarendon Press, 1975), 2, p. 908.

16 S. Freud (1929) Letter to Binswanger. In *Letters of Sigmund Freud* (New York: Basic Books, 1960).

17 Don DeLillo, *The Body Artist* (New York: Scribner, 2001), p. 77.

18 Ibid., p. 126.

19 From her book *Emergence* (Hastings: Reality Street Editions, 2010), p. 13.